Attracting
& Feeding
HUMMINGBIRDS

Stan Tekiela

Adventure Publications
Cambridge, Minnesota

Dedication

To my mother, Adele, who always supports me in my endeavors into nature.

Acknowledgments

Thanks to the Bird Collection, Bell Museum of Natural History, University of Minnesota (St. Paul) and the All Seasons Wild Bird Stores in Minnesota, which have been instrumental in obtaining some of the images in this book.

Thanks also to Jim and Carol Zipp, good friends and wild bird store owners, for reviewing this book.

Credits

Front and back cover photos of birds by Stan Tekiela. Front cover pattern by EVAsr/Shutterstock. Front cover bird icon by mr.Timmi/Shutterstock.

All photos by Stan Tekiela except pg. 39 by Michael A Siino/Shutterstock.com and pg. 42 by Backyarder /Shutterstock. All bird images are Ruby-throated Hummingbirds unless otherwise labeled.

Edited by Sandy Livoti

Cover and book design by Jonathan Norberg

10 9 8 7 6 5 4 3 2

Attracting & Feeding Hummingbirds

First Edition 2015, Second Edition 2022
Copyright © 2015 and 2022 by Stan Tekiela
Published by Adventure Publications
An imprint of AdventureKEEN
310 Garfield Street South
Cambridge, Minnesota 55008
(800) 678-7006
www.adventurepublications.net
All rights reserved
Printed in China
ISBN 978-1-64755-335-7 (pbk.); ISBN 978-1-64755-336-4 (ebook)

TABLE OF CONTENTS

All About Hummingbirds

I can't think of any more specialized, highly adapted birds than hummingbirds—especially Ruby-throated Hummingbirds. Hummers are the tiniest of birds, with some sparrow-sized exceptions. They are the only birds that can fly backward or upside down, hover steadily while feeding, and perform aerial somersaults! Their vibrant plumage is unique in the bird world. The males have glittering throat patches or crowns that not only impress the females but also capture the hearts of many who enjoy watching and feeding birds.

The Ruby-throated Hummingbird (*Archilochus colubris*) is in the Apodiformes order, a huge group of birds that includes hummers and swifts. The hummingbird family, called Trochilidae, has two subfamilies. It includes Phaethornithinae, commonly called the hermits, which are drab, curve-billed tropical birds ranging from Mexico to South America. The brightly colored hummers with shorter, straighter bills in the Trochilinae subfamily are called tropical hummingbirds and live north of Mexico.

The hummingbird family has more than 325 species residing only in North, Central and South America. We have 16 hummingbird species in the United States and Canada combined. Ruby-throats are the only ones regularly found in the eastern half of the United States. All of the others are seen in parts of the West.

male

female

FACTS

Relative Size: the Ruby-throated Hummingbird is one of the smallest of all of our bird species

Length: 3–3.5" (7.5–9 cm)

Wingspan: 4–4.5" (10–11 cm)

Weight: .11 oz. (3.2 g)

Male: green back with a black throat patch (gorget) that changes to brilliant ruby red in sunlight, white-to-gray belly, long and thin black bill, tail is long and projects beyond wing tips when bird is perched

Female: same as male, without the throat patch

Juvenile: same as female; juvenile males may have flecking on the throat

Nest: cup; 1.5–2" (4–5 cm) wide, 1.5" (4 cm) high; female constructs with assorted fluffy plant materials and glues them together with spiderwebs; camouflages the exterior with bits of lichen and bark, seamlessly blending the nest into the supporting branch

Migration: complete migrator; has a consistent, seasonal migration

Food: insects, flower nectar, solutions of water and sugar

RANGE & HABITAT

The only hummingbird found across the eastern half of the United States and into eastern and central Canada is the Ruby-throated Hummingbird. It has the largest range of all of our hummers and is thriving well nearly all environments from Florida to southern parts of Canada.

The other hummer species, shown on pages 10–13, occur in the western half of the country, with some reaching into western Canada. Rufous Hummingbirds range from Alaska to Mexico. Calliope, Black-chinned and Broad-tailed Hummingbirds have the widest ranges in the West. The rest have small ranges and occur mainly in California and Arizona.

Ranges in brown indicate where the birds can be seen during the breeding season. Migration ranges are shown in tan. Hummingbirds move about freely, so you can also see them outside their typical ranges at different times of the year.

RUBY-THROATED HUMMINGBIRD

■ Breeding Season ■ Migration

ALLEN'S HUMMINGBIRD

ANNA'S HUMMINGBIRD

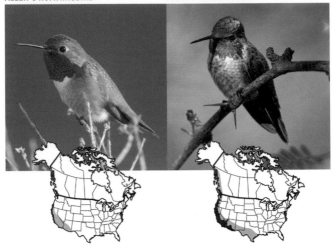

BERYLLINE HUMMINGBIRD

BLACK-CHINNED HUMMINGBIRD

■ Breeding Season ■ Migration

BLUE-THROATED HUMMINGBIRD

BROAD-BILLED HUMMINGBIRD

BROAD-TAILED HUMMINGBIRD

BUFF-BELLIED HUMMINGBIRD

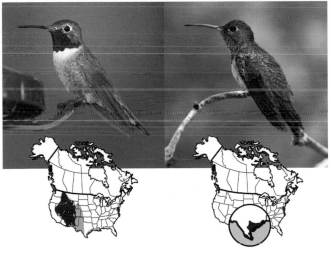

■ Breeding Season ■ Migration

CALLIOPE HUMMINGBIRD

COSTA'S HUMMINGBIRD

LUCIFER HUMMINGBIRD

MAGNIFICENT HUMMINGBIRD

 Breeding Season ▇ Migration

RUFOUS HUMMINGBIRD

VIOLET-CROWNED HUMMINGBIRD

WHITE-EARED HUMMINGBIRD

■ Breeding Season   ■ Migration

CALLS & SOUNDS

Hummingbirds are unique birds with no ability to sing. Instead of singing musical songs to communicate like some bird species, their flashy feathers and remarkable flights do the talking. They make a single vocalization, called a call note, and will chatter or buzz, giving a rapid series of call notes. They will also regulate the volume of the sound from soft and intimate to harsh or loud and aggressive, depending on the circumstance.

A male Ruby-throated Hummingbird establishes and defends his territory with a series of call notes. He moves around the edges of the territory, which ranges from half an acre to a full acre, "marking" the boundaries with a string of harsh vocalizations. If this isn't enough to keep an intruding male from entering his territory, he greets the interloper with a very loud and insistent series of calls along with a visual display of brightly colored, puffed up feathers.

During courtship a male Ruby throat will perform an aerial display flight in front of the female while giving a series of very loud and rapid chip notes. Often these flight notes can be heard from a long distance.

Quick Tips

- The "humming" of a hummingbird in flight is created by its rapidly flapping wings disturbing the surrounding air
- In all hummingbird species, the females are much less vocal than the males
- Well-fed, healthy baby hummers are usually silent
- Male Ruby-throats give strings of loud, fast chip notes during their display flights that can be heard from afar
- Male Broad-tailed Hummingbirds make a noise in flight that sounds like a tiny ringing bell

In general, female Ruby-throats give less harsh call notes than the males. They issue their softer calls when an intruder comes too close to the nest or babies. To avoid drawing any attention to themselves or their nests with eggs or babies, they are often silent when they're away from the nest.

Nearly all of our hummingbirds make a humming noise with their wings when they fly. Their wings are flapping at such an incredibly high rate, from 70–80 beats per second during regular flights to as much as 200 beats per second during chasing or courtship flights, that it disturbs enough air to create a humming sound.

In the United States and Canada, male Broad-tailed Hummingbirds have tapered outer primary flight feathers that produce a trilling sound, which is similar to a tiny bell ringing. Air rushes over these feathers when the male is in flight and creates the sound. The trill announces his presence to females and tells the other males to stay away. As the season wears on, so do his feathers, and the ringing bell sound decreases. By winter it may be entirely gone. This is a distinctive and unique sound that you will not forget if you are fortunate enough to hear it.

Broad-tailed Hummingbird

Black-chinned Hummingbird

NESTS

Like all hummingbird species, female Ruby-throated Hummingbirds build open cup nests. Only year-old females and older will breed. Oftentimes a young female hummer returns to the area where she hatched to find a place to nest. She looks for a good site, adequate food and clean water and will claim the area as her territory only if her mother or other females aren't there. Females start building their nests even before searching for a mate. Sometimes older females repair and reuse their nests from the previous year. There is documentation that one hummingbird nest was used 5 times in 5 years!

Over the next 6–10 days the female brings in a variety of soft plant materials. She usually builds on a nearly horizontal branch that's often less than 3 inches wide. Sometimes nests are built on a forking branch. Most are constructed in shade and tucked under some leaves.

The female builds the base first and binds it to the branch with spiderwebs. Then she constructs the sides and uses her body to shape the interior cup. All nest materials are glued together with spiderwebs. She gathers these by flying through spiderwebs and taking them back to the nest using her bill, chin and belly.

Hummingbird nests are so well constructed that they are said to hold water. The mother makes the nest only big enough to fit her body in snugly, but the spiderwebs allow it to expand. Eventually it will need to enlarge to fit the two growing babies that will be filling the cup.

EGGS, CHICKS & JUVENILES

Ruby-throated Hummingbirds nest up to two times per season. In colder northern states, they usually have time for only one brood. In southern states, where it stays warm longer, they often try to nest twice. Two eggs are typical, but more than two is often the result of a second female laying an egg in another female's nest. Males don't help incubate or raise young. At birth, chicks are naked and helpless and cannot regulate their own body temperature. The mother must continue to sit on them (brood) until they have enough feathers to keep themselves warm. She leaves only to eat and defecate.

Within just 14–18 days of hatching, baby hummers leave the nest (fledge). Now they are juveniles, full size and look like the female. Juveniles tuck into leaves and wait for the mother to feed them. Two weeks after fledging, the youngsters are feeding themselves and will remain on their own until next spring when they return to breed.

Broods: 1–2 per season

Clutch Size: 2 eggs (1–2 average)

Egg Length: .5" (1.3 cm); about the size of a pinto bean

Egg Color: white and unmarked

Incubation: 11–14 days; only the female incubates

Hatchlings: naked except for sparse tufts of down feathers, with eyes and ears sealed shut

Fledging: 14–18 days

HUMMINGBIRD TRIVIA

- The average hummingbird has about 1,000 feathers.

- Hummingbirds are the smallest birds in the world. Bee Hummingbirds are the tiniest, with a length of only 2 inches and a weight of just 1.8 grams. Calliope Hummingbirds are the smallest hummingbirds in the United States, weighing only 2.5 grams.

- Hummingbirds are named for the humming sound created by their rapidly flapping wings.

- More than 25–30 percent of a hummer's weight is the chest (pectoral) muscle, which powers the wings.

- Compared with other birds, hummingbirds have the largest hearts in proportion to their bodies. The heart accounts for 2.5 percent of their total body weight.

- On average, a Ruby-throated Hummingbird weighs 1 gram less than a Bald Eagle's primary flight feather.

- Most hummers live only about 3–5 years. The oldest Ruby-throat lived for 9 years, and the oldest Broad-billed Hummingbird lived to a ripe old age of 12 years.

- Hummingbirds have an excellent memory. They often return to look for food at the exact spot where you put your feeder the previous year.

- Hummingbirds don't suck up nectar with their bills. They have a uniquely grooved tongue that flicks into nectar and laps it up at about 10 times per second.

- Hummers feed on average 7–10 times per hour. Each feeding lasts upwards of 30–40 seconds.

- Hummingbirds consume 5–6 grams of nectar daily. The liquid passes through their digestive system in about 20 minutes, and the sugars are extracted.

- A single hummingbird collecting nectar can visit over 1,000 flowers in just one day.

- Hummingbirds are pollinators for many plants.

- Hummers eat many insects, but unfortunately for us, mosquitoes are too large for these tiny birds to eat.

- The wings (wrists) of hummingbirds are fused and don't bend like the wings of other birds.

- Hummingbirds don't flap their wings up and down like other birds. They rotate their wings at the shoulders in figure-eight patterns, giving them power strokes on both the top and bottom of their wings.

- Hummingbirds are the only birds that have the ability to hover without using a headwind.

- It's not true that hummingbirds never land. In fact, they spend most of their lives perched on a branch near their food source or nest.

- The heart rate of a hummingbird is about 250 beats per minute at rest and can rise to over 1,200 beats per minute during flight. This means the heart can beat from about 4 times per second to more than 20 times per second!

- Migrating hummers can reach speeds of 25–30 mph.

- The Rufous Hummingbird migrates the farthest of all hummers, with some flying more than 2,000 miles from Alaska to Central America and often crossing over several mountain ranges.

- Ruby-throated Hummingbirds fly more than 500 miles nonstop, taking upwards of 24 hours to cross the Gulf of Mexico from Texas to land at wintering grounds in Central and South America. In spring they make the same flight back when they return north to breed.

- The closer to the equator, the more hummingbird species you will see.

- Hummingbirds have great color vision that is about equal to ours, but they also can see in ultraviolet light.

- Male hummingbirds often have a throat patch, called a gorget, or a crown that becomes brightly colored in sunlight and impresses the females during courtship.

- Male hummingbirds have separate territories from the females and don't help with nest building, incubating or raising the young.

Broad-billed Hummingbird

Feeding Hummingbirds

Hummingbirds are insect-eating machines! They snatch up dozens of tiny insects, which are high in protein and fat. Hummers also carefully extract insects trapped in spiderwebs that the spiders haven't devoured yet.

When hummingbirds are not consuming insects, they feed heavily on a sweet, clear, sugary fluid produced by flowers, called nectar. Most flowers have similar amounts of sugar. The flowers attract insects, which accomplish pollination as they go from flower to flower. The payoff for the bugs is a tiny sip of sweet nectar. Hummingbirds also enjoy the high-calorie food offered by the flowers.

Attracting hummingbirds to your yard can be fun and easy. A great first step is to plant a small garden with annual or perennial flowers or cultivate some showy flowers in large pots on your patio. The best way to draw hummers is to choose flowers with long tubular shapes—especially red ones. Ask your local nursery which of these types of plants grow well in your region.

Find a place near the flowers to hang a hummingbird feeder. If no flowers are growing, put a shepherd's hook into the ground or potted plant and attach a red silk flower. Fill a red feeder with a water and sugar solution to mimic flower nectar, and the hummers will come.

HOW TO MAKE HUMMINGBIRD SOLUTION

To make a nectar solution for your feeders, simply use water and white granulated sugar. Do not use brown sugar, imitation sweeteners or honey. These products won't work and can harm the hummers in some cases.

Keep your homemade solution clear and do not add food coloring of any kind. Bright red colors used to attract hummers should be located on the feeders.

Most flowers produce a 20 percent sugar (sucrose) solution. To match this, mix four parts water with one part white sugar. This will make a 25 percent sugar solution that your visiting hummingbirds will love.

In very hot weather, the solution will start to turn cloudy and spoil after several days. Commercial products are available to help extend the life of your nectar solution, but you can retard spoiling by just boiling the mixture for a few minutes.

Allow the solution to cool to room temperature before filling your feeders. Hot solution will not only scald the hummers, but you can also get burned if you happen to spill it while filling. It can crack glass containers and melt plastic containers as well.

If your hummers are finishing the homemade nectar quickly and you are replacing it daily or every other day, you can skip the boiling method. Since the solution won't have a chance to spoil, just dissolve the sugar thoroughly in warm tap water.

FEEDING Q&A

Sugar and sucrose—what's the difference?
Sugar comes in different forms. Sucrose is a simple sugar and an organic compound known as granulated or table sugar. White granulated or table sugar is the only sugar you should use to make homemade nectar.

If a 25 percent sugar solution is good, is a 50 percent solution better?
It's best to try to match what most natural flowers are producing and offering to birds, so the simple answer is no. Studies have shown that hummers can detect very slight differences in sugar solutions. The average hummingbird has only about 10 taste buds (as opposed to the 10,000 taste buds in humans), but each one seems to be tied to detecting sugar. In solution-concentration studies, hummers consistently chose nectar with high sugar content in the natural range of 20 percent.

What if I make too much solution?
Any extra nectar should be stored in the refrigerator. You can keep it in a pitcher or jug so it's easy to pour directly into feeders when you need to refill

You may also freeze extra solution for future use. You can thaw it slowly in the refrigerator or just leave it out to melt to room temperature. Stir the solution before you pour it into feeders and watch the hummers enjoy it.

Will cold solution from the refrigerator harm my hummingbirds?
Some people are concerned that filling feeders with cold solution taken directly from the refrigerator will

make the hummers cold. However, the volume of fluid ingested by hummingbirds during one visit isn't enough to lower their core temperature. Also, the number of calories derived from the feeding offsets the cold liquid. Regardless, it's easy enough to wait just 30 minutes for the solution to warm before pouring it into your feeders.

Should I use ant moats?

Many people who feed hummingbirds have trouble with ants. A simple ant moat works well to keep ants off a feeder. Ant moats are usually cuplike structures that hold a small amount of water or vegetable oil. Feeders hang from the moats and present an impassable surface, which keeps ants off the feeders.

There are also products available on the market for coating feeder poles and other structures that hold feeders and actually repel the ants. After coating, within a day they will give up trying to reach the sweet food.

Rufous Hummingbird

When should I put up my feeders in spring?

Hummingbirds are fairly reliable and return about the same time annually. Depending on where you live, your hummers will arrive sometime after the weather has warmed and the flowers are blooming. Many web pages track the migratory progress of hummers each spring. Check online to gain insight about their location.

What if my feeders go dry when I am away on vacation?

Hummingbirds don't completely rely on your feeders. They use feeders as a supplement to their regular diet. If you go out of town and your feeders run dry, the hummers will simply obtain their nutritional requirements from garden flowers, wildflowers, flowering shrubs and trees and other nearby feeders. They are extremely well equipped to find other sources of food. Simply fill your feeders when you get home, and they will soon return.

Should I stop feeding hummingbirds at the end of summer?

Many people mistakenly believe that hummingbird feeders should be taken down at the end of summer to force the birds to migrate. This action actually removes the best source of food that your hummers have—and just when they need it the most!

Hummingbirds need to feed heavily before migrating to store up enough energy to make the trip. Please keep your feeders up for several more weeks after you see your last resident hummingbird. Migrating hummers passing through may spot your feeding station and will be refreshed by the unexpected nourishment.

Hummingbird Feeders

Glass nectar feeders are great if raccoons, squirrels, bears or other animals aren't trying to get to the nectar. If your feeders are being knocked down by unwanted critters, plastic would be a better choice.

Some people think nectar feeders with no perches are best since they force the birds to hover as they feed, mimicking their natural behavior at flowers. Others believe that perches permit hummers to rest and feed more efficiently. Perches allow many hummers to land and feed while others wait nearby for a port to open.

When just 1–2 hummingbirds are visiting early in the season and you have a large feeder, fill it only partially to avoid spoilage and waste. Small capacity feeders are better for slower feeding stations.

Quick-Tips

- Both glass and plastic feeders trimmed with red work very well to attract hummingbirds
- Glass nectar feeders are slightly easier to clean than the plastic varieties
- Hummingbirds feed equally at nectar feeders with or without perches
- Use window and test tube feeders for close-up viewing
- When making a nectar solution for your feeder, do not add any food coloring

FEEDER TYPES

Jar or Container Feeder:

These feeders are the most common type for hummingbirds. They are simply a glass or plastic bottle or jar attached to a plastic or metal device that serves up sugar water in a simulated flower-like structure. The twist top and neck of these feeders often make them hard to clean. The best ones have wide mouths that allow a bottlebrush to fit for scrubbing.

Plate or Flat Feeder:

These are often flat, plate-like structures with flower-like ports where hummers can feed. They often have a central metal pin or stalk from which the feeder hangs. Usually they have built-in ant moats. They come apart easily, which makes for trouble-free cleaning.

Window Feeder: Typically made of plastic, window feeders for hummers are usually small, clear and trimmed in bright red, with suction cups that adhere tightly to the surface of windows. They are excellent for attracting hummingbirds to watch and enjoy close-up. Window feeders don't hold a lot of nectar and need to be refilled frequently, but they are easy to open and clean.

Test Tube Feeder: These are small, thin plastic or glass feeders shaped like a test tube, usually with a red tip to help attract hummingbirds. They are good for small patios and spaces where large feeders won't fit. Test tube feeders run dry quickly and need refilling often, but they work well to draw hummers to see up close.

Decorative Feeder: Often made of hand-blown glass or similar material. These often look great, but they don't disassemble and there is no way to scrub the inside. They usually don't last more than one season.

Bee Guards: Hummer feeders should have bee guards on their feeding ports. In late summer, when bees, wasps and other nectar-loving insects are more plentiful, it becomes much more important to have some sort of bee guards on feeders to reduce the chances of bees gathering the nectar.

A bee guard is typically a small plastic device that increases the distance from the surface of the plastic flower to the nectar solution. Bees have short tongues and can't extend them more than a quarter inch. Hummingbirds use their long bills and tongues to reach deep into the feeding ports to reach the nectar. Look for bee guards when deciding on a feeder.

Costa's Hummingbird

PLACING FEEDERS

Hummingbird feeders are a wonderful addition to your bird feeding stations. The best placement for these will be different from your seed feeders.

Because hummingbirds are so small, it's best to keep their feeders closer to the house so you can easily see them. Place feeders within 10 feet of the house, but consider applying reflective stickers on the outside of windows and glass doors nearby. Glass can reflect the sky or surrounding area and set up the possibility of hummers colliding with it. Stickers will help avoid this.

Flower gardens are excellent places to begin feeding hummingbirds. They are often already feeding there, so providing them with a constant source of food will be good news that travels fast. Putting up a shepherd's hook to hang a feeder in your garden is quick and easy to do.

Hummingbird feeding stations should be placed near a tree or other vegetation so the hummers can perch on a twig and survey the surrounding area. Feeders close to shrubs or other cover give hummingbirds a place to stage, guard their food source and look for predators before flying in to feed. Plant cover also gives them a quick place to hide in case a hawk swoops in.

When placing hummingbird feeders, be sure to install a squirrel or raccoon baffle on each one. Baffles are metal tubes that prevent animals from climbing feeder poles and shepherd's hooks and accessing the nectar.

Place feeders where squirrels, raccoons and bears can't get to them. For squirrels, the basic placement rule is 5 feet and 8 feet—meaning feeders should be at least 5 feet off the ground and at least 8 feet from any other surface from which a squirrel can jump. This includes trees, houses, sheds, grills, birdbaths, patio furniture and anything else a squirrel can climb to jump on top of baffles and onto feeders.

Raccoons are masters at climbing, but a raccoon-style baffle works well to keep them off a nectar feeder. These should be installed using the same precautions as squirrel baffles.

Bears will tear down just about any feeder, not just nectar feeders. If you live in bear country, the best way to keep these animals from coming into your yard and creating a dangerous situation is to take your feeders in at night.

If possible, place all of your hummingbird feeders in the shade since direct sunlight will spoil the solution quickly. Hummingbirds also like the shade. It provides them with more protection against predators and the heat of the day. Shade keeps their heat levels down while they are working hard to obtain nectar.

Putting out an assortment of hummingbird feeders is always good since a variety helps to attract more hummers. Put up some large, others small, some with perches and others without. Don't forget some window feeders so you can see the birds close-up.

Multiple hummer feeders will bring in larger numbers of hummingbirds. Many feeding stations have upwards of 10 hummingbird feeders. Placing several together will concentrate the birds in one spot. Spreading them out will thin the density.

Hummers are highly territorial and spend a lot of time perching and protecting feeders. With much exertion, they vigorously defend a consistent food source. When they see a visitor try to feed at "their" feeder, they zip out and chase away the interloper.

Putting up more feeders will often reduce the amount of fighting over one feeder and has the added benefit of attracting more hummers. Nevertheless, when you have multiple feeders, you may still see a lot of fighting for a position to sip some nectar. Additional feeders should be placed out of sight from each other since individual hummingbirds seem to dominate individual feeders. Consider putting one feeder in front of the house and the other in the back. This will help reduce conflicts among the birds.

Some great places to hang additional feeders are in the eaves of the house, close to windows. Well-placed hummer feeders just outside your kitchen, living room and home office windows will bring you delight with each and every hummingbird visit. These sites are also extremely good because they prevent squirrels and raccoons from reaching the nectar.

Maintaining Feeders & Good Practices

Feeder maintenance is essential for the overall health of all species of hummingbirds. How often you clean your feeders depends on the heat of the days. Cleaning is more important and must be done more often during the hottest part of summer. Frequent cleaning is not as necessary during spring and late summer.

Whenever you see the nectar solution become cloudy, it is time to clean the feeder and change the solution. There are a number of products on the market that will lengthen the life of the solution even on hot summer days. Most are a liquid preservative that is safe for birds and keeps the solution clear for several more days.

A number of transmissible diseases are associated with birds, including hummingbirds, and their droppings. To be safe, use good hygiene practices and take some basic precautions when filling or cleaning your feeders.

For example, when you clean your feeders, wear rubber gloves. After cleaning, vigorously wash your gloved hands and cleaning brushes with warm, soapy water. Use paper towels to pat dry, and discard the towels.

CLEANING YOUR FEEDERS

Always try to use rubber gloves when handling your feeders and cleaning the feeding area because there are several diseases that can be picked up from bird droppings. *Histoplasma capsulatum* is a fungus in soils that is deposited from bird and bat droppings. Many people who contract histoplasmosis don't develop symptoms, but some exhibit mild flu-like symptoms. Rarely, other people can suffer serious complication

Cryptococcosis is another fungal disease found in the environment, and it also comes from bird droppings. Often associated with pigeon droppings, it is best to wear rubber gloves and a mask when cleaning up scat on feeders and around sites where large numbers of birds gather. Like histoplasmosis, many people don't suffer any symptoms. Some just come down with symptoms of a mild flu.

West Nile virus is carried by mosquitoes. Hummers and other birds contract it but don't transfer it to humans, so there is no need to be concerned about getting this disease from your feeders.

Keeping your feeding station clean and refreshing the site are quick and easy ways to stop the spread of avian disease and other diseases from bird droppings.

For hummingbird feeders, oftentimes all it takes is a simple rinse of the entire feeder before you refill it with fresh solution.

If black mold starts to grow inside or on exterior parts of the container, you should spend extra time scrubbing it off with soapy water. Dismantle the feeder as much as possible and scour the parts with your scrub brushes and cleaning solution. Clean it inside and out and rinse thoroughly with hot water. Bring it to room temperature by running cold water over it, refill the container with fresh nectar solution, and set it out once again for your hummingbirds to safely enjoy.

About the Author

Naturalist, wildlife photographer and writer Stan Tekiela is the originator of the popular Backyard Bird Feeding Guides series that includes *Attracting & Feeding Finches*. Stan has authored more than 190 educational books, including field guides, quick guides, nature books, children's books and more, presenting many species of animals and plants.

With a Bachelor of Science degree in natural history from the University of Minnesota and as an active professional naturalist for more than 30 years, Stan studies and photographs wildlife throughout the United States and Canada. He has received national and regional awards for his books and photographs and is also a well-known columnist and radio personality. His syndicated column appears in more than 25 newspapers, and his wildlife programs are broadcast on a number of Midwest radio stations. You can follow Stan on Facebook, Instagram and Twitter, or contact him via his website, naturesmart.com.